ISBN: 978-1-48359-778-2

Huck's Duck Clucked

Huck's Duck Clucked

by Kelly Day PhD.

Illustrated by Beth Dupree

Co-Illustrated by Will Useman

Dedication

In memory of Fedrick who loved unconditionally.

Kelly Day, PhD.

For my loves, Steve and Sophie.

Beth Dupree

You won't believe your ears,
so listen closely so you will hear;

A story of a boy named Huck
who had a duck that suddenly
clucked.

"Cluck you say?
There's no possible way!
A duck says quack,
even when his name is Jack!"

But not on this day;
Not on Huck's farm;
No, on this day,
the animals were charmed.

This morning was not different,
not different than any other;
Except for this morning,
Huck ran quickly to tell his mother.

"Mother", Huck said,
"How could it be?"
"My duck's not quacking,
he's clucking at me!"

Mother said, "Don't be concerned,
the animals are just taking turns;
They're learning each other's sounds,
so that they can travel around;

Just as we do, when we speak
a different language so that we
can understand,
what people are saying from
different places and faraway lands."

Huck walked outside
and there was the cow;
She didn't say, "Moo",
instead, she said, "Meow!"

The cat smiled at the cow when
the cow made a "Purrrrr";
The cat in return said, "Moo"
and then licked her yellow fur.

In the stable outside,
Huck heard the horse say,
"Bahhhh" to the sheep
and the sheep said "Naaay!"

Out under the tree stood
the donkey and the dog;
The donkey barked and the dog said,
"Hee-haw."

The pig wasn't far away,
with the owl close to the hay;
The owl said, "Oink"
and the pig said, "Who?"

And nearby the goat didn't bother to answer,
but continued to chew.

The goat took another bite
and looked up from his food;
Just as the rooster said, "Mehehehehe"
the goat responded,"Cock-a-doodle-doo!"

As Huck walked toward the pond,
he heard the goose gobble and the turkey quack;
He thought, "Wow, what a day,
I better get back!"

"I have to tell my friends
but they may never believe,
about the day the farm animals
talked to each other
and how they all agreed;

That learning each other's languages
through understanding their sounds;
Taught the animals that they could get
along just like people who open their
minds and find that they are no longer bound;

Instead, when we listen
and care about each other;
We learn that we are all very similar
like sisters and brothers."

Letter from The Author

This book was inspired through mentoring and advocating for African refugees who resettled in the U.S. Although the majority could not speak English, they spoke with their heart through their undiminished faith and love of God. I am humbled, honored, and excited to share this story with you about a little boy named Huck who discovers that even though we may be different and we may speak different languages, we can all get along and love one another.

Kelly Day, PhD.

Letter from The Illustrator

I felt a kinship to this story because of the love of a farm and animals. It was fun creating Huck, giving him expressions as he encountered his farm animals, communicating other sounds than their own. I live with a supportive husband, Steve, and a loveable canine, Sophie, who waited patiently by my chair to go play ball.

Beth Dupree

Letter from The Co-Illustrator

Diversity to me is one of the best parts of life. In this world full of different perspectives we all help each other learn, grow, and appreciate new insights for the benefit of our own expansion. I love that Huck and the animals play as catalysts who harmoniously demonstrate that we're all in this together.

Will Useman